Journey Through the Church Year

The Time
of
Easter

Written by Suzanne Richterkessing • Illustrated by Susan Morris

AID ASSOCIATION FOR LUTHERANS

4321 N. Ballard Road, Appleton, WI 54919-0001
www.aal.org • e-mail: aalmail@aal.org • (800) 225-5225

© 1999 Aid Association for Lutherans

Published by Concordia Publishing House
3558 S. Jefferson Avenue, St. Louis, MO 63118-3968
Manufactured in the United States of America

1   2   3   4   5   6   7   8   9   10   08   07   06   05   04   03   02   01   00   99

Smidge and Smudge were exhausted from learning so many things. They quickly moved into their new home in the big pipe. From the opening in the pipe, they had a mouse's-eye view of everything that took place in the church.

When Smidge suggested they take a late winter's nap, Smudge agreed. Soon they were sound asleep in their new, soft, warm nest.

Umpah, diddle, boom, ding.

"What's that?" Smidge and Smudge whispered loudly.

Umpah, diddle came the sound again.

Smidge and Smudge scrambled out of the pipe as fast as their legs could take them. They hurried across the balcony, down the stairs and around the corner.

Whump!

"Well, hello!" said the familiar voice that had guided them through their first months in the church.

"It's … it's … him again," stammered Smidge.

"Where are you this time?" asked Smudge playfully.

"Here I am! I am Elder Mouse at your service. I have lived in this church for many years. What's your hurry?" he asked, adjusting his glasses.

Smidge and Smudge, each interrupting the other, told Elder Mouse about the loud noise coming from their new home.

"Ah, yes," he said. "I was waiting for you to discover that your new home was in an organ pipe. The organist is practicing for the Ash Wednesday service. Be quick now, I know a perfect place for your new nest. Indeed, indeed!"

Elder Mouse led Smidge and Smudge down a hall and into a room with a large desk, comfortable chairs and shelves of books. They entered a closet where they scrambled over shoes, around boxes and across piles of magazines until they came to an old, well-used briefcase.

"I've had my eye on this briefcase for my new home," said Elder Mouse. "However, I've decided I rather like my old home. You can have this one, indeed, indeed!"

Then Elder Mouse left Smidge and Smudge to explore their new home.

The briefcase was empty except for a piece of carved wood attached to a chain. It was wedged in a corner. Smidge and Smudge decided to ask Elder Mouse about it.

Three days later, Elder Mouse summoned the young mice. "Learning time, learning time," he announced as he settled himself on top of a box Smidge and Smudge had found.

Season of Lent

"The season of Lent begins today, 40 days before Easter," Elder Mouse began. "During Lent there are special church services. God's people come to worship, just like they do on Sundays. They come to hear and think about the story of Jesus. God sent Jesus to take the punishment for people's sins."

"What are sins?" asked Smudge.

"Sins are wrong things that people do or think," said Elder Mouse. "In the Bible, God tells people the things they should and should not do. During Lent, people sing songs and say prayers of thanks that Jesus was willing to die for them so their sins could be forgiven."

Ash Wednesday

Elder Mouse adjusted his glasses. "Lent begins today on Ash Wednesday—"

"Why is it called Ash Wednesday?" interrupted Smudge.

"Let's go see," answered Elder Mouse.

The three mice ran to the church and quietly watched the Ash Wednesday service. They saw the pastor dip his finger in a small pot of ashes and make a cross on the forehead of each person.* As he did this, the pastor said, "Ashes to ashes, dust to dust …"

Elder Mouse told Smidge and Smudge the cross made from ashes would remind God's people that Jesus died on a cross for their sins.

*Note: This practice is not universal. Refer to the parent's guide for explanation.

The cross of ashes made Smidge and Smudge think about the piece of wood in the briefcase. Then they saw the cross above the altar. A purple cloth was draped across the arms. As they looked around the church, Smidge and Smudge saw many crosses.

The weeks passed. Every day Smidge and Smudge learned something new. They learned that the lamb on the altar cloth stood for Jesus, the Lamb of God. They listened as the people sang, "O, Christ, the Lamb of God, who takes away the sin of the world."

Palm Sunday

One Sunday, as Smidge and Smudge were busy tidying up their nest, Elder Mouse paid them a surprise visit. "This is the beginning of a very special week called Holy Week," he announced. "This week God's people will hear the story of how Jesus died and rose again for them. They will come to church many times.

"Today is Palm Sunday," he continued. "The Bible tells how Jesus rode into Jerusalem on a donkey. People were so happy to see Jesus. They waved palm branches and shouted 'Hosanna! Hosanna!' Today, God's people will remember that day, waving palm branches and singing songs to Jesus."

Smidge and Smudge watched the celebration from the balcony with Elder Mouse.

Maundy Thursday

Four days later, Elder Mouse visited the two young mice again. "This is Maundy Thursday," he began. "It is time to remember how Jesus ate supper with His friends. He gave them bread and said, 'This is my body.' Jesus gave them wine and said, 'This is my blood.' God's people come to this special meal, the Lord's Supper, to receive forgiveness and remember that Jesus died for their sins."

Elder Mouse explained that after the special meal, Jesus and His friends went to a garden to pray. After He prayed, soldiers came and took Jesus away. They did not believe He was God's Son.

"At the end of the Maundy Thursday service, everything on the altar is removed," Elder Mouse told them. "This reminds God's people that Jesus' life was about to end."

The three mice watched as the cross and candles were removed from the altar.

Good Friday

Elder Mouse met the young mice the next day and took them back to the altar.

"Today is called Good Friday. God's people come to church to remember the day Jesus died for their sins," Elder Mouse said. "The church is dark. The altar and the cross are covered with black."

"Oh, this is not a happy day," said Smidge. She wiped a tear from her eye.

"It may seem that way, but the good news is that this is only the first part of God's plan," explained Elder Mouse as he placed his arms around Smidge and Smudge. "Something very exciting is about to happen. God will turn the cross from something sad into something happy."

Smidge looked at Smudge, and they both looked at the cross.

"We have something to show you!" they said. Smidge and Smudge described the beautiful piece of wood they had found in the corner of the briefcase.

"My, oh my. Indeed, indeed!" was all Elder Mouse could say. "You don't suppose it could be …"

Elder Mouse asked the young mice to show him their treasure.

Elder Mouse clapped his paws when he saw the piece of wood. "It is, it is! Indeed, indeed!" he exclaimed. "This cross was made in Jerusalem, the place where Jesus died. The pastor always wore it on Easter Sunday. He hasn't worn it for two years because it was lost. But you have found it!"

Elder Mouse decided the three of them should move the cross so it would be found. Smidge and Smudge tugged, pulled, pushed and shoved until the cross was out of the briefcase. They slid it across the floor while Elder Mouse retrieved a piece of yarn from his nest. Then, they used the yarn to hoist the cross to the top of the pastor's desk. Smidge and Smudge positioned the cross in the center of the desk.

Easter Day

On Sunday morning, Smidge and Smudge woke to beautiful, joyous music. The people were singing, "Alleluia! Jesus lives!"

"Today is Easter! On this day, Jesus rose alive from the tomb where He had been buried," Elder Mouse explained. "Now God's people know they will have eternal life. Indeed, indeed."

"What's eternal life?" asked Smidge.

"It means God's people will live in heaven with Him forever."

Smidge and Smudge noticed that the altar was covered with white. They knew it was a special day. Beautiful flowers decorated the church and a banner hung on the wall.

Then Smidge and Smudge saw the pastor wearing the wooden cross! They smiled. They had helped the pastor find the cross. They, too, had played a part in this Easter celebration.

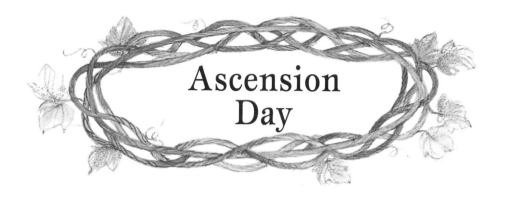

Ascension Day

During the Easter season, Smidge and Smudge listened as God's people rejoiced because Jesus was alive. The Easter season lasted 50 days. On the 40th day, Ascension Day, the congregation celebrated Jesus' going to heaven to prepare a place for God's people.

"Is the Easter season over now?" Smudge asked, his curiosity getting the better of him.

"Ah, the answer to that question is long enough to fill a book. Indeed, indeed!" replied Elder Mouse. He already was making plans for the next things Smidge and Smudge would learn.